Contents

Introduction	**7**
Equipment	**9**
Camera	9
Lens	9
Film	14
Accessories	15
Technique	**21**
Rules of Photography	21
Record	21
Pictorial	21
Action	25
Exposure	30
Composition	67
Flash	71
Night	73
Air-to-Air	73
Subject	**79**
Air Display	79
Airfield	83

Colour Gallery 33 to 64

Lens	33
Filters	36
Pictorial	36
Exposure	41
Night	42
Composition	43
Air-to-Air	45
Subject	47
Air Display	48
Airfield	53
Museum	57
Selling	59
Faults	60

Airport	84
Holiday	84
Museum	85
Filing	**88**
Prints	88
Transparencies	88
Selling	**89**
Markets	89
Research	90
Presentation	90
Fees	92
Faults	**93**
Composition	93
Out of Focus	93
Movement	94
Exposure	95
Flash	95
Colour	95
General	96

▲ Not the most photo-genic aircraft but one of the rarest. This Lockheed F-117 stealth fighter appeared in public only weeks after its existence had been disclosed by the military authorities. It was photographed during the George AFB open day in November 1990.

◄ Do you have the stomach for air-to-air photography? This unkind picture of the author was taken by the base photographer at RAF Alconbury after his air combat sortie in an F-15 Eagle.

A Guide to Aviation Photography

Cover illustrations

Front

Three Pilatus PC-7s of the Martini aerobatic team making smoke, captured with a 70–210mm zoom lens. Note the conformance with the classic rule of thirds. This states that the point of interest should lie at one of the thirds; this is a third of the distance from the top, or bottom, of the picture and a third of the distance from the left- or right-hand edge.

Inset

By excluding the crowd and cars from the picture, this photograph of a replica Bristol Boxkite is timeless. The Boxkite was built for the film 'Those Magnificent Men' and photographed with a 300mm lens. Photographs of aircraft like this are ideal for selling to birthday card agencies and non-aviation magazines.

Back

A 300mm telephoto lens has been used to compress this composition of Farnborough Air Show crowd and the world's largest aircraft, the Russian Antonov An-225.

A Guide to **Aviation**

▲Even when taking air-to-air photographs from an aircraft as steady as a Tornado, a high shutter speed is recommended to reduce the risk of camera shake. Care must also be taken to minimise canopy reflection. The subject here is a Tornado GR.1 from the TTTE.

Photography

T. MALCOLM ENGLISH

ARMS AND
ARMOUR

To Aileen, for her patience and understanding

Acknowledgments: I am indebted to so many people for their assistance in the preparation of this book that, sadly, space precludes mention of them all. I should, however, like to express my appreciation to the many USAF, RN and RAF public affairs officers for the facilities granted me over the years; in particular Mr M. Hill, CPRO of RAF Strike Command. Grateful thanks are due to Mrs K. Langshaw, Mr P. Langshaw, S. Lury and Mr G. Rogers whose photographs are included in the book. I should also like to thank Mr P. Silcock, Ilford Sales Service, and Mr P. Sutherst, Kodak Technical Advice Service, for details of their products, and Ms S. Rapley, Public Affairs Officer, Airship Industries, for a flight in what must surely be the ideal camera platform for air-to-ground photography – the airship.

Arms and Armour Press
A Cassell Imprint
Villiers House, 41–47 Strand, London
WC2N 5JE.

Distributed in the USA by Sterling Publishing Co. Inc., 387 Park Avenue South, New York, NY 10016-8810.

Distributed in Australia by Capricorn Link (Australia) Pty. Ltd., P.O. Box 665, Lane Cove, New South Wales 2066.

British Library Cataloguing-in-Publication Data: a catalogue record for this book is available from the British Library.

ISBN 1-85409-089-5

Designed and edited by DAG Publications Ltd. Designed by David Gibbons; edited by David Dorrell; layout by Anthony A. Evans; typeset by Typesetters (Birmingham) Ltd.; camerawork by M&E Reproductions, North Fambridge, Essex; printed and bound in Great Britain by The Bath Press, Avon.

Introduction

Opportunities to take aircraft photographs, which were once the preserve of professional photographers, are becoming increasingly available to enthusiasts. These include facilities such as photo-calls at military airfields, and public displays of a wide variety of aircraft from the top-secret Lockheed F-117 stealth fighter to the Russian MiG-29 'Fulcrum'. Furthermore, developments in camera technology and mass production have brought cameras and lenses, having 'professional' specifications, within the reach of keen amateurs.

As an example of the advances made in so-called 'snap-shot' cameras, it is interesting to compare my first camera, a Kodak Brownie Cresta, given to me about 25 years ago, with today's equivalent. My Brownie has (I still have it) a fixed shutter speed, fixed focal length lens and a slider which allows a close-up lens or yellow filter to be positioned over the lens. In contrast, modern cameras are fast becoming micro-computers on a strap; electronics taking care of focusing, exposure, winding on the film and even popping up the built-in flashgun if the light is failing.

With cameras having such automation and optical quality to match, it would seem difficult not to take perfect pictures every time. Where do we go wrong? Well, not all of us own such sophisticated equipment and those who do come to realize the truth of the cliché that it is the photographer and not the camera that takes the photograph.

With this in mind, this book is intended to assist and encourage the ever-growing number of enthusiasts who share my love of aircraft and a desire to capture them on film, irrespective of the photographic equipment they own. It is also aimed at photographers turning to aviation as a new subject.

In writing for two groups, which include experienced photographers and knowledgeable aviation enthusiasts, it is inevitable that some of the sections of this book will be familiar. Nevertheless, I hope that photographers will pick up useful snippets of information from the chapters on 'Equipment', 'Technique' and 'Faults', and that aviation buffs will find the chapter devoted to 'Subjects' of some interest.

Aviation photography is little different from any other branch of photography. Consequently, photographers experienced in other branches of the hobby will find that techniques they have mastered are equally applicable when photographing aircraft. In portraiture for example, one of the primary rules is that the subject's eyes must be in focus, whereas landscape photographers are aware of the importance of composition. Accurate or selective focusing and composition are equally relevant to aviation photography.

Try as I may to avoid the use of technical terms, some, such as 'depth of field' and 'f-stop', are fundamental to any branch of photography. Consequently, although they are briefly defined here, I suggest that anyone unfamiliar with them and who is keen to understand basic photographic principles, purchases one of the several, inexpensive 'introduction' books on photography. I can particularly recommend *Starting Photography* by Michael Langford, published by Focal Press Ltd.

Camera clubs are another excellent means of learning about photography. They contain a wealth of experience which members are always keen to share, and offer the opportunity to improve one's standards by entering club competitions. Be warned though, that judges can be less than fully knowledgeable on the subject of aviation photography and it is infra-dig to comment on their criticism. Consequently, you will have to bite your tongue when, having proudly submitted your faultless in-flight picture of a Spitfire, or whatever, the judge utters the immortal words 'Aren't Airfix kits realistic. Did you use a hairdrier to spin the prop?'

Equipment

◀ This Boeing 747, 'Air Force One', was an unexpected arrival to London's Heathrow Airport during a recent presidential visit. The first-ever aircraft photograph taken by Mrs K. Langshaw, it demonstrates what can be achieved by beginners to photography.

◀ A 24mm wide-angle lens was used to include the fuel tanker and Lockheed ER-2. Unless deliberately planned, care must be taken not to get distortion when using such wide-angle lenses.

• **Camera:** Until the advent of affordable single-lens reflex (SLR) cameras, aviation photographers were limited in the pictures they could take by the capabilities of the fixed-lens cameras in popular use. Standard lenses are fine for photographing aircraft on the ground, where access is available, but are too short for most in-flight subjects. It is not surprising, therefore, that the most popular camera for aviation photography is the interchangeable-lens 35mm SLR.

Consequently, this book has been intentionally biased towards users of these cameras. That said, it has been written with other types and formats very much in mind, particularly the less sophisticated viewfinder cameras.

Broadly speaking, there are four types of camera design: direct viewfinder cameras, SLR, twin-lens reflex (TLR) cameras and view and technical cameras.

Direct viewfinder cameras have a viewfinder in the camera body, usually above the lens, which gives a direct view of the subject being photographed. They cover the spectrum of sophistication from disposable and Instamatic cameras, having fixed focal length lenses and single shutter speed, to the famous Leica M series, and compact cameras having an automatic focusing zoom lens with a coupled viewfinder, automatic exposure, motorized film winder and integral flashgun.

As the viewfinder is located away from the lens, you see a different image from that of the lens. At long distances this is not a problem because the images tend to coincide for all practical purposes. However, it can pose problems when taking close-up photographs. A further disadvantage with the less sophisticated models is their single, relatively slow shutter speed (about 1/125 second), particularly when taking action photographs. Their advantages are relatively low price, light weight and, compared with SLR cameras, which incorporate a hinged

mirror, they tend to have a smoother 'taking' mechanism so there is less chance of camera shake.

Single-lens reflex cameras are the most versatile for a variety of subjects, not just aviation. This is due to the wide range of interchangeable lenses which may be fitted to them and because the image seen in the viewfinder is the same as that passing through the lens. Other advantages include the ability to measure the correct exposure, and control the shutter speed and aperture settings. Disadvantages are relatively high cost, bulk and weight, but these tend to pale into insignificance when compared with their flexibility.

Twin-lens reflex cameras have, as their name implies, two lenses, both having the same focal length. One lens is used for viewing and focusing, the other for taking the picture. Consequently, when taking close-ups, TLR cameras suffer from the same problems as viewfinder cameras. A further disadvantage is that the image on the focusing screen appears reversed left to right. This can be most disconcerting when trying to follow a moving subject. This type of camera is now only available in the 6cm × 6cm (2¼in square) size which gives higher quality results than smaller format cameras.

Viewfinder and technical cameras are extremely simple in construction and use individual sheets of film, usually 5in × 4in (12.7cm × 10.1cm). As a result of their large format they tend to be rather unwieldy. A further disadvantage is that the image appears inverted on the focusing screen. In spite of this they are used by a small number of aviation photographers for static subjects requiring the ultimate in image quality.

• **Lens:** Most cameras are purchased with a 'standard' lens. This is normally of between 35mm and 55mm focal length on a 35mm camera and 75mm to 80mm on 2¼in format cameras. These produce the most natural perspective, are often of high optical

◄ The red star on this pilot's helmet symbolizes the role of the USAF's Aggressor squadron. The Aggressors, who were based at RAF Alconbury, simulated a Soviet threat for dissimilar air combat training of NATO aircrew. The photograph was taken with a 70–210mm zoom lens.

▼A 300mm lens was used to compress the distance for this picture of the French Air Force 'Patrouille de France' aerobatic team at the 1990 RAF Alconbury air show.

quality and are eminently suitable for static subjects where the photographer has free access to the subject. However, there are some situations where a lens having a different focal length will be essential. Hence the popularity of interchangeable lens cameras. For example, within the confines of a cockpit, a wider-angle may be needed to include the full width of the flight deck.

Lenses are normally described by two parameters: focal length and aperture – for example, 300mm and f5.6. The focal length is a measure of the magnifying power; a 300mm lens will produce an image on the film six times longer than will a 50mm standard lens. The aperture is the hole behind the lens which determines the amount of light reaching the film. Paradoxically, the smaller the 'f' number the larger the aperture size and thus more light is admitted.

Lenses for 35mm cameras are available in focal lengths from about 6mm ('fish-eye') to 1,200mm, but those at the ends of the range are extremely expensive and are used almost exclusively by professional photographers. Lenses for 35mm cameras are popularly categorized as extreme wide-angle (up to 28mm), wide-angle (28–35mm), standard (35–55mm) and telephoto (above 80mm). In addition, zoom lenses are available covering a variety of focal lengths.

Wide-angle lenses are often of value when photographing in confined spaces, such as cockpits and hangars. They are also useful for static displays, when aircraft are parked close to the crowd line, and for dramatic shots on the approach – when access permits.

Telephoto lenses are particularly useful for action photography – take-off, landing and in-flight – and for taking details of static aircraft. In general, the longer the lens the greater the scope for in-flight shots. However, long lenses are difficult to hold steady. An empirical rule of thumb states that the slowest practical shutter speed is the inverse of the focal length of the lens: for example, 1/50 second for a 50mm lens and 1/500 second for a 500mm lens.

Zoom lenses were, until recently, considered to have noticeably inferior optical qualities to their fixed focal length equivalents. Although prime lenses are still undoubtedly superior, the difference is insignificant for most practical purposes and is more than offset by the ability to change the composition of a picture without moving position or changing lens. The wide range of

▶ Air show organizers encourage set-piece displays such as this by the Royal Air Force of a Spitfire and Tornado. Being rather small aircraft, a 300mm lens was needed to capture decent-size images.

◀Wide-angle lenses can be used to exaggerate perspective, such as the long wings of this Lockheed TR-1. A 24mm lens was used for this photograph, taken at RAF Alconbury, to get all the aircraft in the frame, even though right up against the crowd barrier.

◀A 300mm lens was used to take this photograph of the Bristol F.2B Fighter's machine-gun.

THIS MACHINE MUST NOT BE FLOWN WITHOUT PASSENGER
OR EQUIVALENT WEIGHT IN GUNNERS COCKPIT

◀A 500mm mirror lens was used to photograph the flight-line at Old Warden. This photograph has been included to illustrate that tight cropping can be as acceptable as including all of the aircraft.

▶ With aircraft protected by barriers, a telephoto lens may be essential for photographing details such as this AGM Maverick missile. The Maverick is seen here mounted on the inboard underwing pylon of an F-4G 'Wild Weasel' Phantom.

▶ Air show participants as large as this Boeing B-52 may sometimes be photographed on take-off with a standard lens. Once in flight, however, a telephoto lens is needed to 'fill the frame'.

zoom lenses now available also means that two lenses can cover a continuous range from extreme wide-angle to medium tele-photo – a range that would otherwise need five or six prime lenses, with their attendant cost and weight.

Converter supplementary lenses are a relatively inexpensive means of changing the focal length of a lens to a telephoto or wide-angle/fish-eye. Although inexpensive, the image quality is poorer than that of a prime lens, being less sharp and having lower contrast. There is often a considerable change in aperture setting, a teleconverter reducing the light transmission by two or more 'f' stops.

▶Fighter-size aircraft being displayed at air shows need a long telephoto lens to fill the frame. This Phantom was photographed with a 500mm mirror lens at the 1990 RAF Alconbury air display.

▼Believe it or not, this picture of an RAF Chinook was taken from the ground. It was photographed with a 300mm lens during its display at the 1990 Mildenhall air show. A fast shutter speed, to reduce the risk of camera shake, has almost 'frozen' the rotor blades.

● **Film:** Choice of film depends largely on the subject and why it is being photographed. Will the aircraft be static or might it be moving and are the photographs for personal use or publication?

The reason for taking the photographs will determine the type of film used: transparency (slide), colour negative, or black and white negative. The subject will then decide the film speed. Film speed, indicated on the box as an ISO number, such as ISO 200, is a measure of its sensitivity to light. Both colour and black and white films are available with speeds from about ISO 25 to ISO 3200.

A fast film will record detail in lower light conditions than a slow film. It follows, therefore, that the faster the film the faster the shutter speed that may be selected, or the smaller the aperture. Hence fast film is preferred for action photography and situations where great depth of field is required.

It would appear, therefore, that the faster the film the better. Unfortunately, with the exception of Ilford XP2 black and white film, grain will tend to be noticeable on a 10 × enlargement (an 8in × 10in print from 35mm) with films of ISO 400 and faster. Hence, in general, as slow a film as possible should be used.

It is advisable to standardize on only one or two types of film in order to become familiar with the way in which they respond

▲A steady hand or camera support is needed for low-light subjects such as this Buccaneer in its hardened aircraft shelter. Alternatively a fast film could be used.

to different lighting conditions and exposure tolerance. Film emulsions are now so well developed (no pun intended) that there is little to choose between them. Colour rendering is a different matter. As individuals see colour in different ways, arguments will continue forever on which film gives the 'truest' colour rendering: Agfa, Fuji, Kodak . . . all have their supporters.

As almost all the photographs I take are for possible publication, I use Kodachrome 64 transparency film. In addition to being the preferred colour medium by most publishers, transparency film can be printed in either black and white or colour. My choice of ISO 64 is a compromise between the finer grain of slower films, which would restrict shooting opportunities with a long lens to bright lighting conditions, and the coarser grain of faster film, less favoured for publication. In bright sunshine I can use 1/500 second at f5.6, which is just fast enough to give a reasonable success rate (no noticeable camera shake) with my 400mm lens.

For non-commercial photography, the main considerations as to which type of film to use are the superior viewing convenience and greater exposure latitude of colour print film, versus the arguably better colour quality of transparency film. The choice is yours.

• **Accessories:** Full details of accessories, available for a variety of cameras, can be found in specialist photographic magazines; so in this section I shall simply list those accessories I have accumulated over the years and found to be of value.

○ *Filters:* I have an ultra-violet filter fitted permanently to all my lenses. Its primary function is to absorb ultra-violet rays and thus reduce the effects of haze. It also provides protection for the front element of the lens. For dramatic cloud effects with black and white film, I fit a red filter. Unlike ultra-violet filters, which have no practical loss of light transmission, the red filter requires a 4 × increase in exposure.

○ *Rifle-grip:* Tripods tend to be too ungainly for action still photography – if this is not a contradiction in terms. Instead, I have found that a rifle-grip is an extremely useful aid for supporting long telephoto lenses.

○ *Lens hood:* Most lenses come supplied with a lens hood and some have integral lens hoods fitted. Unless the sun is almost behind your back, a lens hood is necessary to prevent extraneous light reaching the lens and causing flare, which degrades the image.

○ *Blower brush and lens tissues:* These are useful for cleaning dust off lenses and out of camera bodies. It is amazing how hairs and dust accumulate and, like flare on the lens, can severely degrade the image.

○ *Gadget bags:* These come in all shapes

and sizes to fit a variety of equipment. Points to consider when buying a bag are the degree of protection it will afford your camera(s) and lens(es), comfort, weight and additions to your equipment such as another lens.

○ *Motor drives and power winders:* With a motor drive or power winder fitted to a camera, the film will be wound on instantaneously after exposure. Alternatively, the motor drive can be selected to fire the shutter continuously as long as the release button is depressed. This enables you to keep your eye at the viewfinder throughout the firing sequence and also to obtain several exposures in rapid succession (up to six frames per second). The latter is particularly useful when shooting transparency film for syndication.

○ *Exposure meters:* These are built in to most modern cameras. However, if you own a camera with adjustable shutter speeds and aperture setting that is not fitted with an integral light meter, you can use a separate hand-held meter. Whichever you use, care must be taken in interpreting their readings, particularly in conditions of high contrast such as an aircraft against a bright sky. There is much to be said for following the guidelines of the film data sheet, and experience in taking photographs over a wide range of lighting conditions.

○ *Flash:* As aviation photography is essentially an outdoor pursuit, there is little need for flashguns. There are occasions, however, such as in a hangar, museum or cockpit, where a flashgun is needed. From personal experience, subjects such as these nearly always require a wide-angle lens. Consequently, if you are likely to take many photographs of this type of subject, it would be well worth investing in an electronic flashgun having a wide-angle flash capability. Otherwise the edges of the image,

◀ Compare this photograph of an Army Air Corps Westland Gazelle, taken with a red filter, with that below. The filter has accentuated the cloud but areas of red, such as the three panels on the fuselage and the pitot cover, have been recorded almost white. A colour photograph of this aircraft is on page 36.

◀ Compare this photograph of an Army Air Corps Gazelle, with that above, taken with a red filter and the colour photograph.

▲A monopod provides a lightweight and convenient support for static subjects.

▼A tripod was used for this photograph of a Lightning in the Quick Reaction Alert hangar at RAF Binbrook, shortly before the type was phased out of service. The original colour transparency has a strong yellow cast due to the artificial illumination. Note the flare in the bottom left-hand corner of the picture, due to the overhead lights shining directly into the lens.

▶Lightweight aluminium ladders are an increasing sight at air shows to allow photographs to be taken over the heads of the crowd. Why one is being used here is a mystery.

◀A flashgun was used for this photograph of a VC10 tanker's flight-deck, taken with a 35–80mm zoom lens.

where the light intensity falls off, will be dark.

The equipment you buy will obviously depend upon many factors, not least of which are finance and other photographic interests. Over a period of years, and by buying some equipment second-hand, I have acquired two 35mm SLR bodies, a 24mm extra wide-angle, 400mm telephoto, 500mm mirror lens, two zoom lenses (35–80mm and 70–210mm), a power winder, flashgun (with wide-angle lens attachments), tripod, rifle-grip, UV filters, a red filter, blower brush and large gadget bag. If this

appears extravagant, remember that it is effectively a 'professional' outfit and has paid for itself many times over in publication fees.

I should add that for a period of about ten years, when I was starting out in aviation photography, I had photographs published in magazines including *Flight International*, *Air Pictorial*, *Scale Models* and *Photography*, that were taken with much more modest equipment. In fact, my enlarger was constructed from a Duckhams oil can, chip board, scrap metal rod and a Russian camera lens – which cost me a total of £15.

◀A flashgun and 35–80mm lens were used for this photograph of the Icelandic Coast Guard's Fokker F.27 Maritime flight deck. The aperture setting was determined simply by using the calculator on the flashgun, which relates film speed, distance to subject and 'f-number'.

▶Fill-in flash was used with a standard lens for this detail of an F-16's main undercarriage leg.

Technique

◄An Air National Guard LTV A-7 Corsair and the fin of an Italian Air Force Tornado at Goose Bay, Canada. Plaques, such as the one on the hangar, are a useful inclusion to place the photograph.

• **Rules of Photography:** Apart from the pleasure of taking one's own photographs, much of the enjoyment of aviation photography lies in appreciating the styles adopted by other photographers. Well-known examples are the stunning cloudscapes, which are the hallmark of Charles E. Brown, and the dramatic wide-angle, head-on, air-to-air photographs of Richard Cooke.

The variety of style and subject matter adds to the interest in viewing other photographers' work, so the following 'rules' are certainly not intended to be religiously followed at all times. Rather, they have been included simply as guidelines for beginners, from which individual styles will emerge with experience.

• **Record:** This describes photographs taken with the intention of obtaining a clear picture of a particular aircraft. Usually the aim is to include a pleasing composition which shows the serial number and squadron markings or airline livery.

Clarity is of the essence, so a fast shutter speed, or camera support such as a tripod, should be used to reduce camera shake.

Lighting is also important. A bright sunny day can be a help or a hindrance, depending on the relative position of the sun. Ideally the sun should be behind the photographer and if necessary, and time permits, it is well worth returning when conditions are right. Similarly, if colour rendering is critical, the 'warm' light at sunrise and sunset may be unacceptable. If so, a blue colour correction filter may be fitted over the lens.

• **Pictorial:** This is where individualism comes into its own and rules can be thrown to the winds – well, almost. Pictorial photographs are those where the subject is presented in a pleasant, sympathetic composition. The photographs of Charles E. Brown are classic examples.

Pictorial photographs tend to be the opposite of 'record' photographs. The aircraft need not be sharp and the colour rendering should be pleasant, rather than necessarily accurate. Careful use of the light meter is required to obtain the dramatic cloudscapes, landscapes and silhouettes so often used by pictorialists.

Commercially processed colour prints

◄Having passed through a phase of aircraft being toned-down for combat, they now appear in a variety of colour schemes, such as this Tornado F.3 resplendent in No 25 Squadron's 75th anniversary markings.

►A 300mm lens was used to take this detail of the stencils commemorating the Tornado squadron's battle history.

21

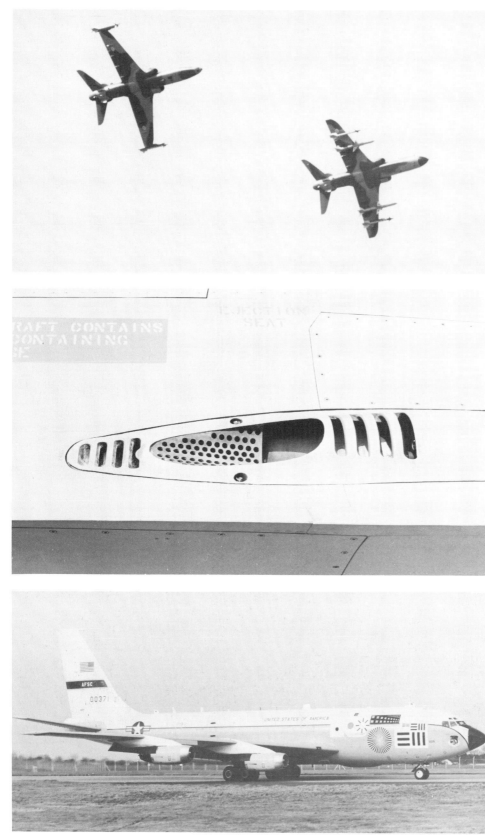

◀ This plan view of a pair of BAe Hawks was intentionally planned to illustrate the variety of weapon fits. The lead aircraft is carrying underwing Sidewinders and BAe Active Sky Flash missiles, while the other Hawk is armed with a pair of wingtip-mounted Sidewinders. With subjects such as this, the aperture must be opened up to compensate for the predominantly light sky area. Otherwise the aircraft would be recorded as silhouettes.

▶ This photograph of the Embraer CBA-123 was intentionally taken in plan view to illustrate the type's unusual engine configuration. It was taken with a 300mm lens at the Farnborough International 1990 air show.

◀ Details of interest to modellers, such as this gun port in the wing root of a General Dynamics F-16, may be photographed with a telephoto lens.

◀ A flying test-card. This Boeing NKC-135A of the Air Force Systems Command was photographed at RAF Mildenhall in April 1989.

▶ A classic record photograph of a Spitfire VC. It was taken with a standard lens at Old Warden, an air show where the organizers arrange the aircraft with photographers in mind.

sometimes lack the impact of the negative. Whenever possible, describe the results wanted to the processor when the negatives are handed in for printing. Otherwise the exposure and colour filtering may be 'averaged' out and lose their punch.

Interchangeable-lens cameras come into their own for pictorial photography; ultra-wide angle lenses can be used for deliberate distortion or to emphasize a distinctive characteristic of the aircraft, such as the high aspect ratio of a glider or the size of a Boeing 747. Alternatively, a telephoto lens can be used to good effect to photograph a selected area of the aircraft.

Examples that come immediately to mind are three-quarter rear view shots of the nose of powerful piston-engined aircraft such as the Hawker Sea Fury. They can even be used to take portraits of the pilot in his cockpit.

Aerobatic teams, with their variety of aircraft, colour schemes and formations, make ideal pictorial subjects. Most teams

◀ The aesthetic beauty of the Spitfire is complemented by the bank angle and cloud as this Mk.XIV turns over the display line at Old Warden. It was photographed with a 300mm lens.

▶ Lightning at dawn. The exposure was based on the highlights in order to eliminate shadow detail, for an atmospheric picture.

▶ The small aperture, which resulted from a high shutter speed selected for this picture of a Sea Harrier, has conveniently thrown the background out of focus. It was taken with a 70–210mm zoom lens.

◀ Lightning halo. This incredible picture was taken at the end of the air show as the Lightning departed for its base through a rain shower. The 'halo' is water vaporizing due to low pressure over the wing and cockpit canopy.

adhere to one or two routines throughout the season, with only minor changes from year to year. Therefore, having seen a previous display, it is a relatively easy matter to plan for the shots you want.

• **Action:** One of the few rules of photography that is sacrosanct states that in order to portray motion, more space should be allowed in front of a moving subject than behind it. Otherwise the edge of the frame ahead of the aircraft appears as a barrier to the motion. Prove it for yourself by using a piece of paper to mask off a photograph of an aircraft in flight.

Ideally the subject should be suitably positioned in the frame at the taking stage. If not, most 'unbalanced' photographs on negative film can be recovered by suitable selective printing. Transparencies can also be improved by masking. This is quite easy to do by judicious use of aluminium baking foil (for its straight edge) stuck on to the slide with adhesive tape; the masked slide should then be held in a glass slide mount.

▲A slow shutter speed, 1/250sec, was chosen to blur the background to this picture of a Swiss Air Force de Havilland Vampire trainer.

▼A Grumman F-14 Tomcat photographed landing on the USS *America*. A fast shutter speed was used to reduce the risk of camera shake and aircraft motion. The resultant small aperture called for careful focusing as there was little depth of field.

▶A fast shutter speed and camera panning were used for this photograph of a Sea Harrier flying off the ski-jump at RNAS Yeovilton.

▶This Jaguar T.2 was used as a photographic aircraft during the Tactical Fighter Meet in 1986. The picture was taken by an envious, earthbound photographer as *Flight International*'s photographer roared off on an air-to-air sortie.

▶This RAF Boeing-Vertol Chinook was photographed during a rapid stop-over to airlift troops into Beirut in 1984. Photographs were almost taken 'on the run' and at such times camera operation has to be second nature. There is no time to fumble with controls or delay over composing the picture.

Depending on the subject, action can be 'frozen' with a fast shutter speed, or the impression of movement can be portrayed by using a slow shutter speed. Usually, when using a slow shutter speed, the camera is panned, thus blurring the surroundings. Alternatively, the camera can be held steady, while the subject moves across the field of view and is itself recorded as a blur. This has been used to good effect when photographing aircraft being catapulted off aircraft-carriers.

Telephoto lenses can be used to take dramatic head-on photographs of aircraft in flight. Furthermore, because the relative speed of the aircraft across the plane of the film is low, a relatively slow shutter speed can be used. This makes for particularly impressive pictures of propellor-driven aircraft, the propellor appearing as a disc.

Contrary to the general advice to use as fast a shutter speed as possible for photographing aircraft in flight, the opposite is recommended for propellor-driven aircraft and helicopters. Speeds of 1/500 second and faster may make the propellor or rotor appear stationary – a most unnatural, not to say unhealthy, condition.

Some photographers use the 'rapid fire' capabilities of motor drives to take sequences of events in the hope that at least one frame will be successful. Although this technique does sometimes work, purists adopt the philosophy preached by Henri

◀ The camera was panned with a slow shutter speed to blur the background of this picture of a General Dynamics F-111 taking off from RAF Upper Heyford.

◀ A 70–210mm zoom lens has been used to include a fellow photographer and a Japan Air Lines Boeing 747. The 747 is seen here on the approach to runway 27R at London's Heathrow Airport. A relatively slow shutter speed can be used for aircraft taken at angles such as this as their relative speed across the plane of the film is quite low.

▲ A Harrier GR.5 in the hover – solves the problem of aircraft movement. It was taken with a 70–210mm lens at Farnborough 1990.

▼ The camera was panned with a slow shutter speed for this photograph of a Jordanian Air Force Dassault Mirage F 1, taking off for the start of its display at the International Air Display, RAF Fairford.

Cartier Bresson that there is only one 'decisive moment'. They shun such hit-or-miss methods, preferring instead to take one photograph at the instant they believe has the strongest visual impact.

● **Exposure:** In order for the photograph to appear as bright as the real scene, the amount of light falling on the film must be correctly controlled by setting the shutter speed and aperture. The brightness of the

subject can be most accurately measured by using a light meter. These are built-in to most cameras now on the market and meter the light through the camera's lens or a window in the body. An alternative is to use a hand-held meter.

Exposure meters are calibrated on the assumption that the subject has an 'average' tone. As most scenes contain a wide range of tones, care must be taken to ensure that

▲Dark backgrounds can fool light meters into over-exposing the subject. Consequently, the aperture was closed down one stop for the photograph of this Swiss Air Force Super Puma.

◀ With subjects such as this, where depth of field is important, the widest aperture setting possible should be used. This will be compromised somewhat by the need for a reasonable shutter speed to prevent camera shake. The aircraft are Tornado GR.1s of the TTTE, RAF Cottesmore.

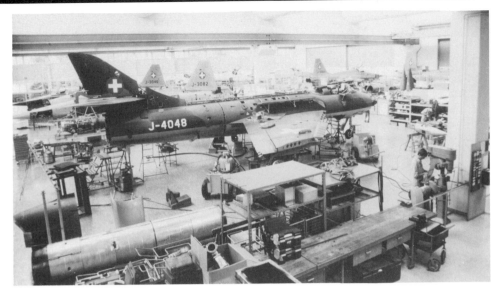

▶ For this photograph of the Swiss Air Force maintenance facility at Interlaken the standard lens was 'opened up' to its maximum aperture of f1.8, to give the fastest

shutter speed and hence reduce the risk of camera shake.

▼ The exposure for this photograph of a Lockheed ER-2 was

based on an average meter reading of the cockpit interior.

Consequently unimportant detail has been burned-out.

the metered area is as close to an average tone as possible. To do this you must first be aware of exactly what area of the scene your meter is measuring. Some light meters consider the whole area and take an average; others measure a small circular area in the centre of the frame (spot meters); while some measure the whole area and bias the average for the light intensity of the central area.

Some subjects may not contain an average tone area at all: for example, an aircraft against bright sky, or a close-up detail of a dark aircraft, such as the Lockheed TR-1. In situations such as these, there are two methods of determining the correct exposure. Either find an alternative (substitute) mid-tone subject, or take a meter reading of the scene and adjust the exposure to compensate for the brightness or darkness.

Judging the degree of correction will come mainly with experience, but as a guide – for an aircraft occupying a small area of the frame with a bright sky background – increase the recommended aperture setting by one or two stops. Conversely, where the scene is particularly dark, such as the example of the TR-1 detail, stop down the lens by one stop. Remember, the exposure recommended by the light meter will give a correct reproduction of a mid-grey tone. If in doubt, bracket the exposures, opening up and closing down the aperture setting, or shutter speed, about that which you estimate to be correct.

With a fully automatic camera, where the shutter speed and aperture are set by the camera, exposure compensation may still be possible by setting the film speed dial to a faster or slower ISO rating than is in the camera. For the bright sky background example mentioned, the film speed should be set to a half or quarter of that in the camera. If you are shooting with ISO 400 film, then the setting should be ISO 200 or ISO 100. Do not forget to return it to the correct value for 'average' subjects.

A good alternative to a light meter, particularly when metering can be impractical or misleading as in air-to-air photography, is to use the guidelines given in the film packaging for a range of lighting conditions and adjust them based on experience.

For simple cameras with fixed shutter and aperture settings, the exposure is predetermined. This precludes using transparency film as its exposure tolerance is too small. Hence the need to use print film, which has sufficient latitude to cope with the non-optimum exposure settings. For lighting conditions most likely to be encountered in aviation photography, an ISO 200 film is a good compromise.

◀This photograph of a Thunderbolt, Mitchell and Mustang could have been taken 50 years ago rather than at one of the many air shows around the country. A 300mm telephoto was used, the aperture being opened up to compensate for the predominant area of light sky.

◀Rotor downwash can be strong enough to blow you over at distances as close as this, so a fast shutter speed is recommended to minimize the risk of camera shake. A disadvantage, however, is that too fast a speed will make the rotors look stationary.

Colour Gallery

Lens

▶A 24mm extra-wide angle lens was used for this self-portrait. Taken in an English Electric Canberra T.4, the exposure was based on that for an average subject in bright sunlight. The Canberra is a less than ideal aircraft for air-to-air photography, having an extremely confined cockpit.

▶Telephoto lenses enable close-ups to be taken of aircraft on the flight-line at air shows. This Sopwith Pup was photographed at Old Warden, using a 300mm lens.

◀▲Some small aircraft require an extremely long lens to fill the frame, when they are in flight. A 500mm mirror lens was used to photograph this Lockheed T-33.

◀Although a telephoto lens is needed for most in-flight photographs, large subjects such as this Boeing 747 and space shuttle can be taken with a standard lens.

▲'As seen on television'. A 300mm telephoto lens has compressed the distance between the A300 Airbus and television aerial to give this dramatic picture.

▶A 70–210mm zoom lens was used for this close-up of the gun and gunsight on the Shuttleworth Collection's S.E.5A.

Filters

▲Compare this colour photograph of an Army Air Corps Westland Gazelle with the black and white prints on page 16. The effect on colour rendering of fitting a red filter can be clearly seen.

Pictorial

▼An unusual view of the Swiss Alps, taken with a 24mm lens from the back seat of a Swiss Air Force Pilatus PC-7 trainer as it banks through 90°. Note the reflections of the pilot's helmet in the canopy.

▲ A slow shutter speed, necessitated on this occasion by the low light level, and panning the camera portray speed as the Deperdussin takes off on one of its rare flying displays at Old Warden.

▼ Things are not always what they seem. This Canberra in the markings of the prototype aircraft was photographed 40 years after the event, during an anniversary meet. Muted colours transform what would otherwise have been just a plain 'record' shot.

▶Colour photography
need not be gaudy to be
successful, as this almost
monochromatic picture
of a Hawker Hind
proves.

▲ Slow shutter speeds are desirable when taking propellor-driven aircraft in flight, otherwise the propellor appears to have stopped. A rifle-grip is a useful accessory to reduce the risk of camera shake. The aircraft is a Spitfire VC, photographed at Old Warden.

◄ A 400mm lens was panned for this photograph of a USAF McDonnell Douglas F-15 Eagle. Telephoto lenses are essential for this type of photograph. The diagonal composition suits the film format.

▲Who has not tried to take a photograph of the two 'Red Arrows' Hawks as they cross during their opposition manoeuvres? Even though a shutter speed of 1/500sec was used, the upper aircraft is blurred. The camera was panned on the lower aircraft.

Exposure

▶If the light meter reading of this Lockheed TR-1 pilot had been used to set the shutter speed and aperture, the picture would have been over-exposed. The aperture was reduced by two stops to allow for the darker than average subject.

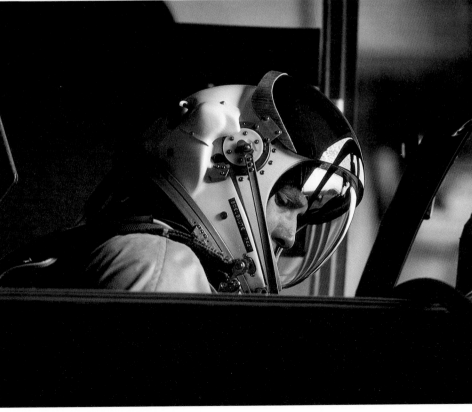

◀For this picture of three BAe Bulldogs silhouetted against a setting sun a 'straight' meter reading was used.

Night

◀Night and low-light photography requires the camera to be held steady during the long exposure times. A tripod and cable release was used for this photograph of an RAF BAe 125. The exposure time was of the order of 20sec.

◀The camera was supported on the island of the aircraft-carrier USS *America* while the shutter was kept open for several seconds to record this picture of a Grumman F-14 Tomcat catapult shot at midnight. The vibration was caused by the ship shaking as the catapult shuttle hit the end stop.

Composition

▲It is sometimes useful to include surrounding details, as in this photograph of a Royal Air Force Lockheed TriStar at Penang airport. The convention of having the aircraft pointing into the picture has been broken, but has been made acceptable by balancing it with the dark figures on the right.

▼A 28mm wide-angle lens was used with a low viewpoint to fill the frame with this General Dynamics F-16 of the USAF's 'Thunderbirds' aerobatic team.

Air-to-Air

◄An archetypal air-to-air photograph of a Panavia Tornado GR.1 from the TTTE (Tri-National Tornado Training Establishment). The exposure settings were based on those recommended in the film data sheet for average subjects in bright sunlight. Had an exposure meter been used, the aperture would have had to be opened up by one stop to compensate for the large area of bright sky. It was photographed from another Tornado GR.1 which, with its high performance, smooth ride and large clear canopy, makes an excellent camera platform.

▲Gliders can be the most difficult subject for air-to-air photography. This is because, unless the photo aircraft can fly at precisely the same speed, it tends to pull ahead. The sortie then necessitates a number of slow flights past the subject aircraft. This Grob Viking was photographed from a Slingsby Venture motor-glider over Syerston.

◀The tower and pier were deliberately included in this photograph of a Pitts Special, as the company which owned it operate out of Blackpool airport. Detailed pre-flight planning is essential for photographs such as this. The photograph was taken using a 35–80mm zoom lens, from a Cessna 172.

Subject

▼Film sets can offer opportunities for photographers forward enough to ask permission to take pictures. This was taken at Duxford during the filming of 'Memphis Belle'.

▲This Belgian Air Force Dassault Mirage 5 was photographed being refuelled at the 1986 Tactical Fighter Meet, RAF Waddington. Unusually the base opened its doors to the public for a photo-call. Details of such opportunities are advertised in specialist aviation magazines.

Air Display

▼The Royal Air Force's 'Red Arrows' aerobatic team photographed with a 70–210mm zoom lens. Manoeuvres such as this can be anticipated by noting earlier displays; they seldom change much.

▶Parachutists, such as the Royal Air Force 'Falcons' parachute team, and hot air balloons are colourful subjects. Their low speed make them easy to frame in the viewfinder.

▼This Avro Vulcan is the last of its type still flying. It was photographed with a 300mm telephoto lens at the RAF Mildenhall air display in 1988. Many enthusiasts get blasé at the frequent display aircraft, such as this. It is only when they are no longer around that they realize how few, if any, good photographs they have of the type. The moral is 'take them while you can'.

◀This photograph of a MiG-29 'Fulcrum', photographed at the 1988 Farnborough Air Show, epitomizes the spin-off to aircraft enthusiasts of glasnost. The emblem on the

Antonov An-124 in the background has been included to emphasize the Soviet connection.

▲Military air shows provide a wide variety of subject matter, often

featuring some of the oldest aircraft in service, to the latest. This Rockwell B-1 bomber, photographed on take-off at the RAF Mildenhall Air Fete in 1989, is an excellent example of the

latter. A 70–210mm zoom lens was used, with a shutter speed of 1/500sec.

▼A dramatic picture of a Royal Netherlands Air Force General Dynamics

F-16 photographed at the RAF Abingdon Battle of Britain air display, 1990, with a 500mm mirror lens. Note the wing-tip smoke generators.

◀ A Boeing KC-135 with refuelling boom extended, photographed at one of the annual RAF Mildenhall Air Fetes. The boom operator's station at the rear of the aircraft is an excellent position for taking in-flight refuelling pictures.

Airfield

▼◀ This Lockheed F-104G Starfighter, photographed at Wittmundhafen, Germany, is one of many gate guardians at military airfields. Note that permission is usually required to take photographs of them.

▶ This is typical of the type of photograph that can be taken at any small airfield. Ask permission to take photographs and keep well clear of aircraft movements. The Tiger Club Stampe SV-4C biplane was photographed at Little Snoring airfield, with a standard 50mm lens, during an aerobatic competition.

▼ Photographing aircraft on the approach to airfields can be rather like fishing; the aircraft do not always materialize. Nevertheless, pictorial photographs may still be possible, such as this winter scene of the approach lights at RAF Cottesmore.

▼Despite their dependence on the weather, airships are still competing with conventional aircraft and helicopters for a number of roles, particularly observation with the police and military. They also make excellent camera platforms for air-to-ground photography. The Airship Industries Skyship 500 was photographed in front of the huge airship hangars at RAF Cardington, from the public road, using a 70–210mm zoom lens.

G-SKSC

◀A typical example of the photographs that can be taken at the approach end of any international airport runway – assuming of course that the laws of the land allow photography at such places. This is a Boeing 737 of the Spanish airline Viva, photographed at London's Heathrow Airport in the summer of 1991.

▲Photographs such as this Tornado GR.1, taken in a valley in north Wales, have to be composed and focused in seconds. Operating your camera controls has to be second nature, otherwise the opportunity is missed.

Museum

◀Museums are an excellent source of material and few are better than the Air & Space Museum, Washington. A 28mm wide-angle lens was used with a shutter speed of the order of 1/8sec to take this photograph of the North American X-15. The slight colour cast is due to the artificial light.

▶Aircraft are seen in the most unusual and unexpected places, so it pays always to have a camera to hand. This is where compact cameras come into their own. This precariously perched Cessna, advertising a shopping mall, was photographed near Fort Worth, Texas.

...ATE RELEASE
...E: A GUIDE TO
AVIATION PHOTOGRAPHY
AUTHOR: T. MALCOLM ENGLISH
CONTACT: KATHARINE SMALLEY
Contact Publicity 212-532-7160

Fax 212-213-2495

LEARN THE SECRETS OF TAKING GREAT AVIATION PHOTOGRAPHS!

For the photographer who wants to improve his aviation shots right away, here's down-to-earth, easily understood guidance. A GUIDE TO AVIATION PHOTOGRAPHY (Arms & Armour, distributed by Sterling, $16.95 paperback) is packed with hints, tips, and advice, all backed up with excellent examples of a variety of aviation topics for study--and the possible results!

Whether you're in the air or on the ground at an air show, you'll have plenty of advice on:

- equipment choices
- gauging weather and light conditions
- choosing prime locations for your best shots
- avoiding basic errors
- specific problems encountered in photographing aircraft
- and much more!

Excellent photos of successful frames--and even "bad" snapshots that show you common mistakes to avoid--illustrate the do's and don'ts of photographing planes on the ground or in flight. Various styles are shown in detail to help you develop and improve your style, and there are even tips on how to market your photographs for profit. In addition to practical, effective, and complete guidance, you'll enjoy the collection of great aviation photography--black-and-white and color photographs of helicopters, light aircraft, commercial airliners, and military fighters soaring across the pages.

****SECOND SERIAL RIGHTS AVAILABLE

TITLE: A GUIDE TO AVIATION PHOTOGRAPHY
AUTHOR: T. MALCOLM ENGLISH
PRICE: $16.95 paperback ($22.95 in Canada)
ISBN: 1-85409-089-5
SPECS: 96 pages (32 in color) * 7 1/2 x 9 3/4
ILLUSTRATIONS: 105 black-and-white
PUBLICATION DATE: February 17, 1993

Please send 2 tear sheets of review to Publicity Dept.

Sterling Publishing Co., Inc.

387 Park Avenue South ▪ New York, NY 10016-8810

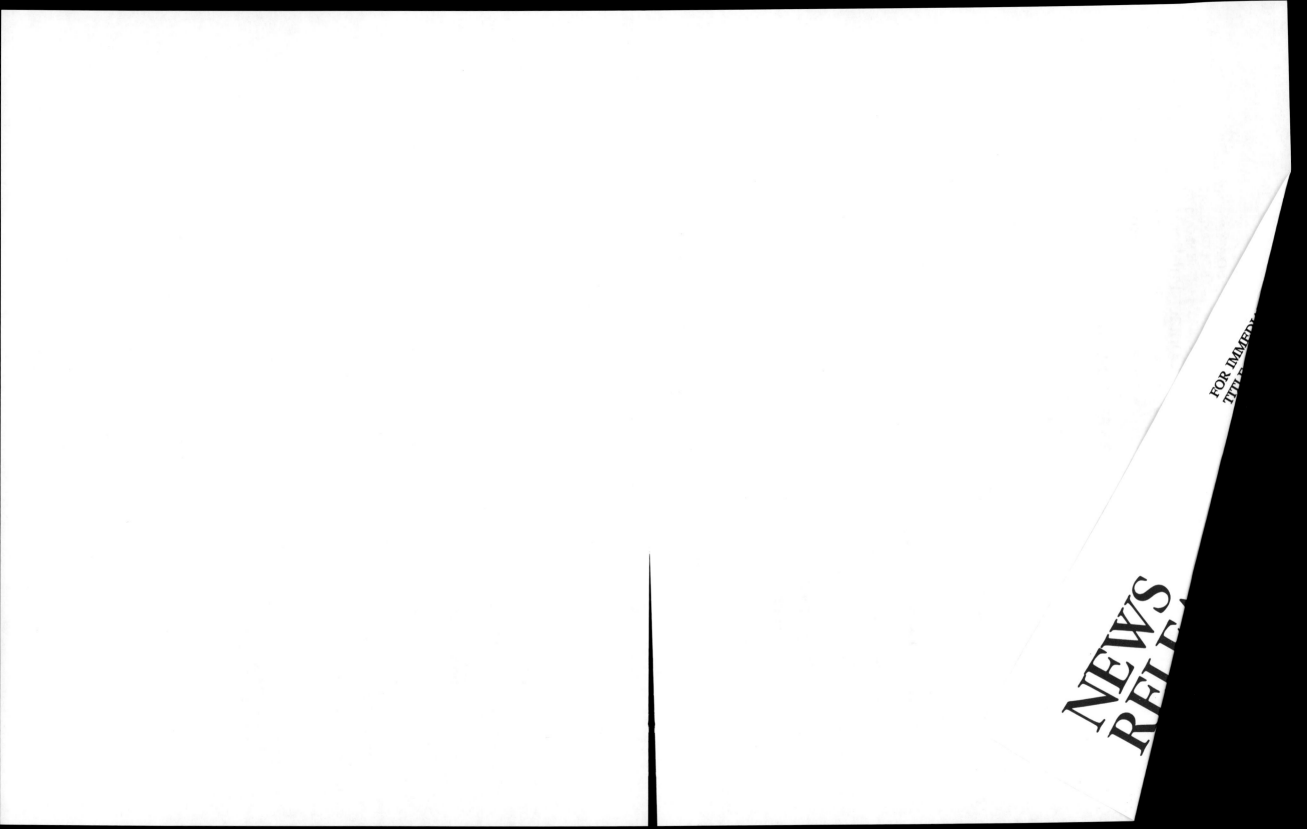

Selling

◄Nose art, as seen on this RAF Buccaneer which participated in the Gulf War, makes an interesting and colourful subject. This machine was photographed at the RAF Alconbury Air Fete in 1991.

▲Try to include human interest in some of your pictures. This photograph of a Boeing E-3A AWACS was taken at the RAF Mildenhall Air Fete in 1990. The vertical format suits this subject, emphasizing the radome, and is useful for book and magazine covers.

◀Photographs of aircrew can often be used to supplement illustrated features for aviation magazines. Pilot and navigator are seen debriefing immediately after a sortie in a Grumman Intruder from the United States Navy flight-test centre, Patuxent River. A wide-angle lens is often preferred to give a mood of intimacy, but this is not always possible. This was taken with a 70–210mm zoom lens.

▶Beware of reflections when taking photographs through glass. They can be minimized, or eliminated, by holding the lens as close to the glass as possible. This was taken from the departure lounge at St. Louis Airport.

Faults

▼Lack of adequate depth of field has thrown the Canberras at the far end of the line out of focus. The picture was taken at a celebration of the Canberra's 40th anniversary.

▶▼ This photograph of a Tornado at night demonstrates how the light intensity from a flashgun decreases with distance. The aircraft was at a distance of about 24m (80ft).

▲With aircraft on the ground there is a tendency to frame them horizontally; a mistake where aerodynamic braking is employed, as here by an F-16 of the 'Thunderbirds' display team.

▼Be prepared for the frame to fill rapidly when using long focal length lenses. The size of aircraft formations are particularly difficult to predict.

▲By not leaving sufficient space in the frame in front of this Swordfish, the slide mount forms a barrier preventing it from flying on.

▼An otherwise excellent photograph spoiled by not being aware of the figures in the foreground as the camera was panned.

▲Fine for a recognition competition, but otherwise disappointing. The solution to small images such as this is to use a long focal length lens. A 400mm lens is recommended with 35mm format cameras for most air shows. The aircraft is a SAAB Viggen.

◄A Royal Norwegian Air Force Hercules seen through a yellow veil. The yellow filter had inadvertently been left on the lens to accentuate cloud by a photographer thinking he had black and white film in the camera.

▲The light level in this hangar at Reykjavik enabled a fairly fast shutter speed to be used for this photograph of the Icelandic Coast Guard's Fokker F.27 Maritime.

▼Dramatic view of a Sukhoi Su-27 at Farnborough 1990, taken with a 500mm mirror lens. The exposure was based on an average subject in bright sunlight. A meter reading from the sky would have under-exposed the aircraft.

▲The Shuttleworth Trust's Bristol Fighter being flown at Old Warden, Bedfordshire. Photographed with a 300mm lens, the head-on view has minimized the effective speed of the aircraft, allowing a slow shutter speed to be used. Note the blurred propellor.

▼It is unusual to get plain backgrounds such as this when aircraft are on the ground; usually they are cluttered with buildings and other aircraft. These Jaguars were photographed taxiing for take-off at RAF Coltishall and have been closely framed by using a telephoto lens.

▶ A 24mm lens and low camera viewpoint were used to frame the Hercules C.3 with the nose probe of the Royal Aerospace Establishment Hercules W.Mk.2.

▼ A 70–210mm zoom lens was used to fill the frame with this General Dynamics F-16. The photograph was taken at RAF Lakenheath at a photo-call during a NATO exercise.

- **Composition:** Aircraft photographed side-on at ground level tend to be rather unexciting. Being long and thin, their geometric proportions are less than ideal for film formats. There are of course many situations where the photographer has little or no control over the positioning of the aircraft and his access. Even so, it is often worth raising or lowering the camera angle. With a viewfinder and SLR camera this usually means lying on the ground or standing on a ladder. Lightweight step ladders are becoming a common sight at air shows to photograph over the heads of spectators.

Where the photographer has some control over the subject, such as may occur at an airfield with light aircraft, time should be spent walking around the aircraft for the best camera angle. A three-quarters front or rear view is often more dynamic than a staid side aspect, particularly when photographed from a low viewpoint.

At the risk of stating the obvious, the composition will be determined largely by the purpose for which the photograph is being taken. If the photograph is intended to illustrate an air show, then it may be beneficial to show the subject amongst other participating aircraft. Similarly, the location of where the photograph was taken may be important, so be aware of control tower or passenger steps bearing the name of the airport. On the other hand, if it is for a personal record, you may wish to isolate it from surrounding aircraft.

Access to a high viewpoint will often allow both types of photographs to be taken by using a wide-angle and telephoto lens respectively. Ladders, colleague's shoulders, control towers, car and hangar roofs are all worth considering as means of elevating the camera. I have even used a helicopter, but that was a luxury.

When more than one aircraft are to be included in the picture, try varying the composition. In addition to photographs which include all the aircraft, try using the closest aircraft to frame those behind it. This technique is particularly useful when comparing two models of the same type of aircraft, such as the fighter and reconnaissance variants of the Phantom. The different nose profiles can be emphasized by framing one by the nose of the other.

In situations such as this, care must be taken to ensure that all the aircraft are in focus. When the lens is focused on a particular point, there is always an area of acceptably sharp focus in front of and behind it. This is known as the depth of field and is dependent on the focal length of the lens, aperture setting and camera-to-subject distance. It increases with small apertures, greater camera-to-subject distance and inversely with increase in focal length. Some cameras have a depth of field preview button which, as its name implies, allows the

◄A high viewpoint was found in one of the maintenance hangars at RAF Abingdon to take this photograph of Jaguars. The depth of field available with wide-angle lenses was useful and the camera was supported on a balcony for the long exposure necessary.

◄By exposing for the highlights, shadow details of these Bell HueyCobra helicopters have been lost, giving a dramatic silhouette.

▶ The diagonal composition, with space in the picture for this formation of Lightnings to move into, gives a dynamic and well balanced effect.

▶ An unusual view of the flight-line at the Swiss Air Force base of Sion was achieved by standing in the cockpit of a Pilatus PC-7. Obviously permission has to be obtained before even touching aircraft, let alone entering them.

▶ A low camera viewpoint has been chosen to emphasize the Lockheed P-3 Orion's distinctive magnetic anomaly detector boom and to frame the other aircraft on the flight line at Keflavik, Iceland. The two aircraft nearest the camera were on deployment from the Royal Netherlands Navy.

▲A low camera viewpoint gives a pleasing composition for a pair of USAF Fairchild A-10s. They were photographed at a photo-call at RAF Lakenheath during a NATO exercise.

▼Looking more like a plastic kit than the real thing, this Canberra was photographed from a Royal Navy Lynx helicopter. A fast shutter speed was used to minimize the risk of camera shake.

photographer to view the depth of field at the taking aperture. The depth of field may also be gauged by the depth of field scale which is marked on some lenses.

Some simple 35mm cameras have fixed-focus lenses with no control over depth of field. However, most of these have wide-angle lenses which give a depth of field from about 2 metres (6ft) to infinity.

Instamatic and 35mm cameras are designed to be held horizontally at eye level, so it is hardly surprising that most photographs taken with these cameras have horizontal formats. This also suits the long thin proportions of aircraft. If the photographs are being taken for publication, look for opportunities to compose a picture with a vertical format. If sufficiently eye-catching and in colour, it may be selected for the front cover. If not, it will give the layout artist a foil to the many landscape format pictures he will have to accommodate.

Try adding human interest by including aircrew or groundcrew; even airshow spectators can sometimes improve the composition.

● **Flash:** Flash-light is particularly useful for interior shots such as cockpits, hangars and in museums. As mentioned in the section on equipment, most of these situations call for a wide-angle lens which in turn needs a flashgun with a compatible light spread.

Flash is normally synchronized to work with camera shutter speeds of 1/60 second or slower. The aperture setting is determined by the power of the flashgun, the film speed

▲ A vertical format was used to concentrate attention on the A-10's Gatling gun and nose art.

▶ A 28mm lens was used to compose this photograph of General Dynamics F-16s visiting RAF Bentwaters.

◀ The distinctive delta wing of the Vulcan was used as a frame for this touching photograph of the scrap dump shortly after the type had been withdrawn from service.

◀ A 300mm lens was used to 'fill the frame' with the three Pitts Special biplanes of the Rothmans aerobatic team. Care must be taken with subjects photographed against a bright sky to ensure that the exposure meter reading is suitably compensated.

◀ A 24mm lens was used for this photograph of a Lockheed TR-1 on the approach to land at RAF Alconbury. The unusual angle was achieved by crouching in the grass.

▲This night-time photograph of the Royal Aerospace Establishment Lockheed Hercules W.Mk.2 required an exposure of approximately 15sec, during which the camera was supported on an engine starter trolley. In addition to holding the camera steady, the lens had to be protected from the rain.

and the flash-to-subject distance. Some flashguns are automatic and will adjust their light output to suit the camera's aperture setting. Others have a set of guide numbers which give the aperture setting for a given film speed and subject distance.

To calculate the aperture setting ('f' stop) divide the guide number, for the film speed you are using, by the flash-to-subject distance. Thus, if the guide number is 88 and the flash-to-subject distance is 8ft, the aperture setting is f11. Take care to use the correct units of distance for the guide number.

In cases where the camera-to-subject distance exceeds the capability of the flashgun, the aircraft can be illuminated by the flashgun off the camera. To do this the camera is left with the shutter open and the flashgun fired by hand at a distance from the aircraft determined by the guide number and aperture setting. For even illumination, the flashgun can be fired several times around the aircraft, although it is important to keep out of the field of view of the lens.

Flash can also be used to lighten shadow detail when the contrast is high. To achieve a natural picture, the 'fill' light should be substantially less powerful than the light it is supplementing. An easy way to achieve this is to set the aperture for correct exposure of the area in direct light, the flash-to-subject distance as described above, and then reduce the flash intensity by placing a handkerchief over the flash tube.

● **Night:** Long time exposures are an alternative to flash photography at night and under low-light conditions, provided that your camera shutter has the ability to stay open for as long as its release is pressed. In many ways this technique is preferable to using flash as it retains the atmosphere. It is possible to measure exposures at night using a sensitive meter, but even this must be factored to allow for reciprocity failure. This is a law which is applicable for extremely long or short exposure times, where the film requires an increase in exposure.

Consequently, exposures at night are usually a matter of guesswork. With luck, the subject will be lit by high-powered floodlights, enabling a meter reading to be used as an estimate. As a rough guide, to expose 'correctly' a subject having a meter reading of 10 seconds, open up the aperture by 1½ stops. Bracketing the exposure time is advisable and you should take at least two more exposures, doubling and halving the time. With such long exposure times a tripod, or other suitable support, may be needed to hold the camera steady.

● **Air-to-air:** To many photographers, air-to-air is the ultimate in aviation photography, capturing aircraft in their natural element against backdrops of cloudscapes, sea or land, and from almost any angle imaginable. Although many of the techniques are common to those used when taking pictures from the ground, there are three 'musts' which are specific to air-to-air photography: flight safety must be paramount; all participating pilots must be experienced in formation flying; and the flight must be planned in detail before take-off.

In the cold light of day it may seem that emphasizing of the crucial importance of flight safety is superfluous. However, once airborne, having invested a lot of money on the sortie – in aircraft, film and time – it is too easy for safety to be sacrificed for 'one more shot'. Be warned!

Ensure that all participating pilots are skilled in formation flying. Most military pilots are, but the chances are you will be flying with civilian pilots and very few PPL holders are trained to fly in formation. Do not assume that the pilots are experienced; if in doubt ask.

Pre-flight planning is essential, not only for safety, but also to brief the pilots on the pictures you want to achieve. Sketches of the pictures you would like to take are useful briefing aids and can be used for route and formation planning. Unless flying with experienced service or display pilots, it is wise

to keep the sortie simple. Even straight and level in echelon with the subject aircraft rocking its wings can produce a pleasing variety of photographs. Variations on this theme are gentle formation turns and changes in height of the subject.

Points to consider when choosing a camera aircraft are obstructions, such as struts, removable window or door to obviate reflections and, most important, compatible performance. Some variation in performance is allowable as I have successfully photographed a Spitfire and Jet Provost from a Cessna 172; an attempt to photograph a Sea Prince from a Cessna 150 was less successful. Because of the speed difference, it was planned to fly opposing race-track patterns, photographs being taken of the Sea Prince when it overtook. The aircraft then split, formating again 360° later. This worked reasonably well until another Cessna transitted our area and was followed by . . . guess what?

Equipment should be kept to the minimum, but do not skimp on film. Whenever possible I take two 35mm SLR camera bodies

▼Cockpit canopy reflections were avoided in this picture of three Lightnings by taking them through the open hatch of a Hercules. Although the relative airspeed was almost zero, a fast shutter speed was used to minimize camera shake caused by the wind buffet in the hold of the Hercules.

▶A pre-requisite to flying in RAF fast-jets is that passengers, including of course photographers, undergo a short aeromedical course at RAF North Luffenham. The highlight is being subjected to hypoxia in the altitude chamber. Hypoxia (shortage of oxygen) is insidious and can be fatal; hence the opportunity to experience it under controlled conditions.

▼A Swiss Air Force Alouette III helicopter against the magnificent backdrop of the Alps. It was photographed with a 70–210mm zoom lens, from another Alouette. Although helicopters have wonderfully large clear canopies, they also vibrate a lot and so a fast shutter speed is desirable to minimize the risk of camera shake.

▲Reflections such as these off cockpit canopies can be reduced by holding the lens as close to the canopy as possible; but it should not touch, otherwise vibration may cause camera shake. The F-15 Eagle and F-5 were photographed from an F-15, using a 35–80mm zoom lens.

◀This dramatic photograph of a Victor tanker was taken from a Victor receiving fuel. A 24mm lens was used, the picture being taken between the pilot and co-pilot. During this delicate manoeuvre, care had to be taken not to disturb the aircrew.

(one for insurance) with 35–80mm and 70–210mm zoom lenses. A motor-drive is a useful accessory, allowing full attention to be paid to the subject without the inconvenience of manually winding on the film.

If it is necessary to shoot through the cockpit canopy or other glazing, make sure that it is cleaned before take-off. Avoid reflections by keeping the lens as close to the glass as possible. With some aircraft, such problems can be alleviated by removing the passenger or cabin door. Alternatively, con-sider shooting through the clear-vision panel that is found on many light aircraft and gliders.

One of the advantages of air-to-air photo-graphy is that although the aircraft may be flying at high speed, their relative velocity will be low. However, fast shutter speeds are still advisable to reduce camera shake due to high-frequency vibration which is present in most aircraft. Care must therefore be taken not to let the camera or lens rest on the structure, such as the cockpit canopy.

▶This unusual view of a USAF Boeing E-3 AWACS was photographed with a 35–80mm lens from the boom-operator's station of a USAF KC-135 tanker.

▼This air-to-air photograph was taken from a Cessna 150, shortly before the Spitfire FR.XIVC was exported to Chino, California. Because of the unfamiliarity with the aircraft, its new owner was unhappy to formate too close to the Cessna, so a 70–210mm lens was used at full extension.

▲'Just feel those muscles'. A 70–210mm lens was used for this photograph of a Lockheed TR-1 pilot chatting to the crowd at the RAF Alconbury air show in 1990.

▼There is no mistaking where this photograph of the Douglas Dakota flight-line was taken. The International Air Tattoo is justifiably proud of its claim to be the largest military air show in Europe. The only criticism is that the close spacing required to get all the aircraft in the confines of the airfield make photography very difficult. A wide-angle lens is a 'must'.

Subject

▼Yet another way of taking unobscured photographs of aircraft surrounded by air show crowds. These enthusiasts are taking pictures of the Sukhoi Su-27 'Flanker', at Farnborough in 1990.

● **Air Display:** During 1990 more than 260 air displays were held in Europe and the United States. They varied in size and participation from informal light aircraft 'fly-ins' and military 'open house' displays to the Oshkosh EAA Convention, which has upwards of 2,000 aircraft on show each year and is attended by some 800,000 people.

To take full advantage of air displays, it is advisable to arrive early and be prepared to stay behind until the majority of visitors have left. These are the times when you are most likely to have the opportunity of taking uncluttered photographs of the static display. A wide-angle zoom (35–80mm) is often the best lens for aircraft in the static park. Allowing yourself a full day will also give maximum variety in the direction of lighting. If colour rendering is critical and the lighting is too warm first thing in the morning, or as the sun sets, fit a pale blue filter to balance the light.

Unless you have specific priorities, it is usually advisable to photograph the largest aircraft first as these tend to be the most difficult to take without people intruding. Details, such as squadron markings and weapons, which can easily be photographed from the crowd barrier, are best left until last. Although you will probably want to exclude people from most of your photographs, it is often worth taking one or two views of the show, with crowds and sideshows. These are likely to increase in interest over the years, relating the exhibits and styles of the period.

The traditional place to photograph the flying display is the runway threshold area. This is where the aircraft are stationary for a while prior to take-off and where they flare for touch-down. It is also probably one of the closest spots on the crowd line to the runway. With a few exceptions, however, photographs taken here tend to be rather unimaginative and static. Although this is fine for 'record' shots, a point approximately mid-way along the runway is better for more dynamic photographs.

As far as possible, aim to position yourself in line with where the aircraft have just lifted off. Of course, not all aircraft will rotate at the same point but, with experience, a good compromise position can soon be established. This also places you nearer to the display datum, which is often close to the centre of the crowd line. Perhaps the most

◀Antonov An-225, the largest aircraft in the world, landing at Farnborough where it was displayed at the 1990 show. This is one of the few aircraft where a wide-angle lens can be used for ground-to-air photographs.

◀This Portuguese Air Force Fiat G-91 was appropriately painted for the Tiger Meet at the 1991 International Air Tattoo and photographed with a standard lens.

◀A Piper Cub carrying out a truck top landing at North Weald is reminiscent of the barn-storming days. A 400mm lens was used to fill the frame.

important consideration of all, however, is to try as far as possible to avoid having to shoot into the sun.

At most air displays, the minimum focal length lens needed to obtain a reasonable size image is 200mm. However, you may find that this limits in-flight shots to side-on views. For greater scope, such as aircraft climbing away and head-on, a 400mm lens is more useful.

● **Airfield:** Both civil and military airfields can offer a varied collection of aircraft. Not surprisingly, civil airfields usually offer the greatest freedom, often allowing photographs to be taken of aircraft in flight or on the field. In-flight photographs are best taken on the approach – that is down-wind of the runway in use. The optimum location for approach photographs can be found from a large-scale map of the area, or a drive around the airfield. The presence of other photographers will usually confirm the 'right spot'. Arriving at RAF Marham many years ago, for the arrival of a deployment of Boeing B-52 Stratofortress bombers – which I thought was a well kept secret – I was amazed to find not only a couple of hundred fellow enthusiasts but also an ice-cream van!

Many civil airfields offer the facility of photographing aircraft on the field, from car parks or viewing areas. If you want to enter the aircraft parking area, it is essential to obtain permission from the air traffic control authority. At no time should you walk near the runway in use or near taxiing aircraft.

Military airfields are another matter altogether. It goes without saying that all signs displayed around the airfield, such as those stating 'crash gates are not to be obstructed', must be obeyed. In Britain, the Official Secrets Act is less than clear on the subject, although under no circumstances must one set foot on the airfield itself without permission. As a general rule, there should not be any problems so long as your photography is restricted to the aircraft and care is taken not to include any of the airfield buildings. In practice this means keeping your back to the airfield and photographing aircraft on the approach.

Some bases, particularly those of the United States Air Forces Europe (USAFE), will

▼Care should be taken when photographing military aircraft from the public highway not to include airfield installations. This picture of an RAF Vickers VC10 K.3 tanker on approach to land is an example of how this has been achieved. Whenever possible keep your back to the airfield.

◀This de Havilland Gipsy Moth was photographed at the annual Moth Meet, held at Woburn Park in Bedfordshire. This is one of the many small light aircraft meets around the country. It was taken with a 135mm lens.

◀This Air National Guard A-7 Corsair was photographed on the approach to RAF Wittering, during one of the Guard's regular deployments. In spite of security restrictions, prior notice of such visits is often published in aviation magazines.

provide guided tours for groups from recognized organizations such as the Royal Aeronautical Society, Women's Institutes and photographic societies. This is an excellent opportunity to photograph aircraft in their working environment. Requests should be addressed to the Station Public Affairs Officer.

If you followed the plight of the British aircraft spotters arrested a few years ago in Greece on charges of spying, you should not need warning about the folly of photographing aircraft (military or civil) abroad. It is not worth the risk; if in doubt, do not photograph. In any case, there has been so much foreign participation at European and American air displays in recent years that there are few fresh types still to see.

● **Airport:** Airliners make colourful subjects and can easily be photographed in flight, while on their landing approach, or static, from the public observation areas within the airport itself. Advice for taking photographs at and around airports is the same as that given above for airfields. The main difference is that you are unlikely to obtain full access to the aircraft.

● **Holiday:** For those fortunate enough to fly to a holiday destination, photographs taken at the airport can provide an interesting introduction to your holiday photograph album or slide show. It is often possible to go 'up front' and have a look in the cockpit. If you do get this opportunity, ask for permission to take your camera and fit as wide-angle a lens as possible.

Contrast on the flight deck will probably exceed the film's tolerance. If you expose for the cockpit interior, the outside detail will be over-exposed; conversely, correct exposure for the outside view will under-expose the cockpit. If flash is allowed, you can use fill-in to balance the contrast; otherwise expose for the subject of greatest interest.

Air-to-ground photographs are often best taken with a wide-angle lens. Do not worry if this means that the engine nacelle or wing tip protrudes into the field of view; they may add interest. Minimize reflections by keeping the lens close to the window and, if possible,

wear a dark, plain top. I had some wonderful air-to-air photographs spoiled by the reflections of my striped shirt.

Holidays are also the time for photographs of opportunity. Low-level jets racing through the Welsh valleys and Lake District can make particularly dramatic photographs if you are fortunate enough to be in the right place at the right time. If you are enjoying a beach holiday, you may see search and rescue helicopters on practice sorties or on routine patrols around the coastline. But although they may make interesting subjects, stay well clear if they are involved in a real rescue mission. Shortly before writing this section, I read in my daily newspaper of a cliff-top 'snap-shotter' who obstructed the rescue of a young girl lying injured at the foot of a cliff. He was so close to the cliff edge that the helicopter crew were afraid he would be blown off by the rotor wash.

● **Museum:** A few years ago it was realized that many aircraft had disappeared from service use and been destroyed without even retaining some of the more famous ones for posterity. As a result, a number of new museums have been created to supplement those already in existence which have an interest in preserving our aviation heritage.

Among the museums in Europe and America, too numerous to mention, are those specializing in aviation, such as the Air & Space Museum, Washington. Others such as the Science Museum in London, although not dedicated to aviation, contain a number of exhibits of interest to the photographer and enthusiast alike.

There are few limitations, if any, to photography although some may prohibit the use of a tripod. Indoor exhibits, lit by artificial light, may also result in peculiar colour casts if using colour film. The Museum Curator or your local camera dealer should be able to advise you on the type of filters to use to correct the colour balance. Alternatively, use a film balanced for artificial light.

Some museums are prepared to open their doors outside normal hours for organized groups, such as camera clubs and aviation societies. This affords the opportunity to take pictures without the usual hordes of visitors being present and you may even be allowed special facilities, such as access to cockpits and inside protection barriers.

▼Holidays provide a source of aircraft photographs. This Royal Navy Westland Wasp helicopter was seen practising cliff rescues in Cornwall and was photographed from a healthy distance with a 70–210mm zoom lens.

▲Aircraft and military museums provide a wealth of material for the aviation photographer. This Victor was photographed with a standard lens, at the Imperial War Museum, Duxford.

▶▲There are several interesting aviation museums. This photograph of an Avro Lancaster bomber was taken in the Royal Air Force Museum at Hendon. A standard lens was used and the lighting is adequate for hand-held exposures on medium-speed film.

▶Shortly after this photograph was taken, the Meteor and Vampire of the Royal Air Force's 'Vintage Pair' display team were destroyed in a mid-air collision. Another example of not passing up opportunities to take photographs; the type will not be there forever.

Filing

Photographers intending to market their photographs will need a quick reference and retrieval system for their pictures. So, although a chore, it is a useful discipline to record and file photographs as soon as they are processed.

I record my photographs on a pro-forma held in A4-size loose-leaf binders and filed alphabetically by aircraft type. Each photograph, in my case 35mm transparency, is given a reference number. This is marked on the transparency holder with an indelible pen. Negatives can be similarly referenced.

Information on the pro-forma consists of: slide reference number, type of aircraft, mark of aircraft, serial number, date and location of where the photograph was taken, attitude of the aircraft and comments. To reduce the amount of space required for all this information, I use codes for location and attitude. For example, 'YVN' is shorthand for Yeovilton, and 'GTT' stands for ground, three-quarters tail. Well, I understand it.

Personal computers with a database software package are ideally suited for this sort of work and will allow selective retrieval.

• **Prints:** There are several ways of filing prints: by type, loose in boxes with the content clearly marked on the box; in transparent sleeve albums, or mounted in traditional albums. As my photographs are primarily for selling, I keep my prints in boxes for ease of retrieval. The choice is yours. Negatives are best filed in transparent sleeves, held in loose-leaf binders with their contact sheets.

• **Transparencies:** As with prints, there are a number of products on the market for filing transparencies. They include trays, which can be loaded ready for use in the projector, slide boxes in a variety of shapes and sizes, and transparent sleeves. I use the latter, with metal bars to suspend the sheets in a filing cabinet. The sleeves can also be filed in a loose-leaf binder.

Before filing your pictures in whichever system you find most suits your purpose, be ruthless in sorting out unsuccessful photographs. This hurts, particularly when it means throwing out photographs of your favourite aircraft, but if you do not do this you will soon run out of storage space. You will also find that as your standards and ability increase with experience, you will wish that you had been more critical from the outset.

Selling

▼A humorous picture of a cheekily stencilled Westland Wessex helicopter (with a Sea King in the background) photographed at a Farnborough Air Show. Subjects like this are unique and have to be grabbed quickly. Therefore focusing, composition and exposure have to be second nature.

● **Markets:** One only has to peruse the shelves of a good newsagent to appreciate the potential afforded by the number of specialist aviation publications. On a recent visit to my local branch of W. H. Smith, for example, I counted fifteen aviation magazines and three modelling magazines, most of which are published monthly and rely heavily on material submitted by readers. In addition, there are a number of aviation/defence magazines which are sold on subscription only and so do not appear in the newsagents. Details of these can usually be found from advertisements in other specialist magazines.

Of course, it is not only aviation magazines that publish photographs of aircraft. There are potential outlets for the innovative aviation photographer in many other specialist magazines, as a study of them will show. Other users of aviation photographs include newspapers, company 'house' magazines, poster companies, calendar and postcard agencies, and book publishers. Fellow aviation enthusiasts on the lookout for photographs of their favourite aeroplane provide yet another outlet, particularly in the United States, where enthusiasts are prepared to pay a commercially acceptable price.

All photographers seriously interested in selling their work are strongly recommended to invest in a copy of the *Writers' and Artists' Yearbook*, and *The Freelance Photographer's Market Handbook*. Both are indispensable

sources of information on a wide range of journals and book publishers, including details of their requirements and payment.

• **Research:** Anyone with a passable knowledge of aircraft and the ability to use a camera has the potential to make money from photography. The difficulty is in identifying the markets and submitting appropriate material.

Analysis of the market is essential, not only to determine the subject matter published by the magazine (book publisher, calendar, or whatever), but also the medium and style. Does the publication use colour, black and white or both; does it prefer 'record' shots or pictorial; single photographs or a spread?

Answers to all these questions can be obtained from a careful study of the market. After which, it is a relatively simple matter to identify the publication(s) featuring the type of photographs you take. Alternatively, if selling photographs is your primary interest, then the results of this market survey will enable you to determine the range and style of subjects published.

Researching the market can be alleviated to a large extent by selling photographs through an agent. As their title implies, picture agents sell pictures; lists of agencies, and details of the subjects they handle, are contained in the reference books mentioned above. Agents typically charge a 50 per cent commission rate for photographs sold. While this may seem high, it must be appreciated that an agent will promote your photographs to many more markets than you are likely to have access to.

• **Presentation:** Having analyzed the market and found an outlet which you feel may use your material, it is then up to you to sell yourself. Following an air show, or the arrival of a well publicized and interesting visiting aircraft, magazine editors will be inundated with photographs. How do you make him choose yours?

It goes without saying that your photographs must be correctly exposed, sharp and clean. They must also be correctly captioned and contain your name, address and, if possible, telephone number. I use self-adhesive labels; an alternative is a personalized rubber stamp.

Most magazines and book publishers are happy to accept original 35mm colour transparencies, preferring these to duplicates and colour prints. Black and white prints should be unmounted, on gloss paper, no larger than 8in × 10in (20.3cm × 25.4cm). Most calendar and postcard publishers require transparencies with a minimum format of 2¼in square, although about 30 per cent will accept 35mm.

While on the subject of submitting original material, be warned that – from personal experience – the majority of transparencies published are returned damaged. There is also a real danger of the material being lost

▼Photographs of aircraft in their working environment, such as this Swiss Air Force Northrop F-5, are useful subjects to have on file for publication by aviation magazines. The inclusion of people in the picture often adds to the interest of an otherwise 'static' photograph.

in the post and by the publisher. I have even had another photographer's pictures sent to me in error, in spite of being clearly labelled with his name and address. With this in mind, it is worth shooting several frames for syndication.

Your photographs should be accompanied by a short covering letter offering the photographs for reproduction at the magazine's usual rate, and a caption sheet. The captions should be typed and concise; with a brief description of the subject and stating where and when the picture was taken. Ensure that your photographs are protected in the post by stiff card; slides should be in glassless mounts and presented in transparent sleeves for protection and ease of viewing.

On behalf of editors, I should add that they appreciate a self-addressed envelope for returning your material – hopefully after use. Some editors will send you a card notifying you of safe receipt of your pictures; if you have not heard after two weeks, it is worth a telephone call to ask if your material has arrived safely.

If you are fortunate enough to obtain a 'scoop', ignore the above procedures and get your photographs to the newspaper or magazine as soon as possible. Telephone the editor first, to explain what you have

▶ How else could Santa arrive at Old Warden than by de Havilland Moth? On occasions such as this, with a group of people, it pays to take several photographs in order to get everyone looking in the right direction. There is always one who doesn't!

▶ Photographs showing the crowds and general views of air shows are likely to be of interest, particularly in years to come for their historical value. This picture of Farnborough 1990 was taken with a 35–80mm zoom lens.

photographed, confirm his interest, and ask his advice on how he wants the material delivered. In exceptional cases the editor will arrange for the film to be processed.

● **Fees:** Before rushing out to order your Porsche in anticipation of a sale, be warned that, with the exception of staff photographers, there are few people, if any, who make a living solely from the proceeds of aviation photography. From personal experience, publication fees per photograph range from zero (and the magazine concerned kept the original transparencies) to £200. Compared with other branches of photography, such as advertising, such pitifully low fees reflect the rules of supply and demand. There are some enthusiasts willing to see their work published for no more than an acknowledgment and many enthusiast magazines are run on a shoestring.

That said, it is satisfying to see one's photographs in print and any payment helps to offset the expense of materials and travel. While on the subject of expenses, all payment received from the sale of photographs must be declared to the tax authorities. This income can, however, be offset by justifiable expenses.

◀This shot of a Lightning had been planned for months as a corny but apt photograph to illustrate an article entitled 'The End of the Lightning'. It was taken from another Lightning, over their last operational base, RAF Binbrook. Cropped to a vertical format, it was used as the magazine cover photograph.

◀A 70–210mm zoom lens was used to photograph the fin markings of this Canberra of No 100 Squadron, RAF. Photographs such as this are a 'must' to accompany magazine articles on a particular squadron or aircraft type.

Faults

▼This photograph of a British Aerospace Hawk is typical of the disappointing pictures taken by beginners. The aircraft often look in the viewfinder to be much larger than they appear on the print. The solution is to be more aware of the size of the aircraft, in the context of the viewfinder image and if possible invest in a telephoto lens.

● **Composition:** One of the greatest causes of disappointment to the beginner is the image size on the print or transparency, particularly those of aircraft in flight. The aircraft that filled the frame when the shutter was pressed somehow appears to shrink during processing and emerges little bigger than a pin-head on your print or transparency.

I suspect that the main reason for the smaller than expected image is 'blinkered' concentration on the subject, without retaining an awareness of its perspective in the viewfinder. The solution is to be aware of the whole scene as it appears in the viewfinder.

Sloping horizontals are another common fault with beginners to photography. It is usually caused by the camera moving as the shutter is pressed. So hold the camera firmly, press the shutter slowly (do not jab it) and keep an awareness of what is in the view-finder.

When taking static or action photographs, try to retain an awareness of people and objects in the immediate vicinity of the subject. Countless photographs have been spoiled by someone or something appearing in the field of view just as the shutter release is pressed.

● **Out of Focus:** Many modern cameras have auto-focus lenses; the most sophisticated can even predict where a moving subject will be at the instant the shutter opens. However, clever as they are, these lenses can still be fooled by objects moving between camera and subject, low contrast subjects, and when photographing through glass. Experimentation is the only sure way to determine your camera's limitations.

At the other end of the technological spectrum, the most simple cameras have fixed-focus lenses which are usually designed to give a depth of field from about 2m (6ft) to infinity. So, unless taking a close-up detail, all aircraft should be in focus. Blurred pictures are therefore more likely to be due to camera shake.

It is not unknown for commercially processed photographs to be printed out of focus. This can be checked by viewing the negatives through a magnifying glass. If the negatives are sharp, demand that they be reprinted.

Action photographs taken with manual focusing lenses can pose a problem. For take-off and landing shots some photographers pre-focus on the point along the runway where the photograph is to be taken; others, including myself, prefer to follow the aircraft and continuously adjust the focus as necessary. With viewfinder-type cameras, it is usually best to pre-focus,

▲This photograph of the solo 'Patrouille de France' Alpha Jet, during an inverted flypast, has been spoiled by extraneous light fogging the film. It was the last frame of a length of film loaded using a bulk film loader.

◀Loudspeaker systems are a hazard at air shows and care must be taken when panning the camera not to spoil photographs such as this of a Boeing B-17 Fortress.

making the maximum use of the depth of field scale.

● **Movement:** This can be caused either by camera shake or subject movement. The former has occurred when there are signs of blur all over the picture. It can be cured by taking care to hold the camera steady, using as fast a shutter speed as possible, and

smoothly pressing the shutter release.

With subject movement, some parts of the pictures are sharp. Risk of subject movement can be reduced by using a fast shutter speed, panning the subject, and photographing it as it moves towards or away from the camera rather than across the viewfinder. When panning the subject, care should be taken to continue the pan while the shutter release is pressed.

● **Exposure:** If the subject, particularly aircraft in flight, appears in silhouette, it is probably due to the exposure meter being biased by the dominating mass of bright sky. As described in the section on technique, with cameras having manual exposure settings this can be alleviated by taking a meter reading from a convenient alternative (substitute) subject. Alternatively, use the settings given in the film data sheet for the appropriate lighting conditions. With cameras having automatic exposure systems, the camera can be fooled by setting the film speed to a lower ISO value. Alternatively, with cameras having an exposure compensation system, this can be set accordingly.

Exposure errors can also occur at the printing stage, particularly if there are extremes of contrast such as an aircraft in flight, as described above. When you think that this may be the cause, do not hesitate to ask the processing company for advice,

and request that the negatives be reprinted.

● **Flash:** If a photograph taken with electronic flash has a section missing, with a straight hard-edged obstruction, it is probably due to the shutter speed being set too fast. Most flashguns are designed to be synchronized for camera shutter speeds of 1/60 second or slower.

● **Colour:** Colour casts can be caused by a number of factors, including:

(1) Time of day; the light at dawn and dusk can be particularly warm.

(2) Outdated film, or film that has been subjected to high temperatures, can suffer from a change in dye quality. It is therefore worth storing unexposed film in a refrigerator and having it processed as soon as possible after use.

(3) Artificial light; daylight colour film is balanced for daylight colour temperatures. When used to photograph subjects illuminated by 'artificial' light such as tungsten or fluorescent, the subjects will exhibit a strong

▼Without protective barriers it is extremely difficult to take unobstructed photographs. Be prepared to arrive early or depart when the crowds have gone home. This Sikorsky SH-3H Sea King was photographed at the Miramar Naval Air Station air day in 1986.

colour cast. This can be eliminated by using a colour correction filter or artificial light film.

(4) Incorrect filtering when printing. If your prints have a colour bias and none of the above factors is applicable, it may be due to incorrect filtering during printing. Ask for your negatives to be reprinted.

● **General:** A couple of classic faults with non-SLR cameras are: no image at all – the lens cap has not been removed; blurred object obscuring the photograph – finger, camera strap or camera case is in the field of view.

A completely blank film is the result of the film not winding on. Take care when loading the film and note that the rewind spool rotates as the film is wound on.

Light areas on the photograph, usually at the edges, are often the result of extraneous light falling on the film. They usually occur at the beginning of the film, when insufficient frames have been wound on.

'Tramline' scratches on the negative are caused by grit on the pressure plate. Dust and grit can be removed by judicious use of a blower brush.

Low contrast, particularly with photographs taken towards the sun, is caused by lens flare. This can be prevented by using an efficient lens hood.

Vignetting (dark corners) of the print is often caused by too long a lens hood or too many filters, which protrude into the field of view.

◀ The thin black line above the hangars is due to a scratched negative, probably the result of grit in the felt light trap of the reusable film casette. There are proprietary 'scratch removers' on the market for slides and negatives that fill in the scratch with a substance having a similar refractive index to the emulsion and they can be extremely effective. Rubbing 'nose grease' in the scratch has similar results.

◀ Although dramatic, this photograph of a Phantom of No 74 Squadron suffers from camera shake. This was due to a combination of long lens (400mm) and jerky panning as the aircraft pitched up rapidly, at high speed.